Short ish Walks
St Ives to ^ Padstow

David Wright

Bossiney Books

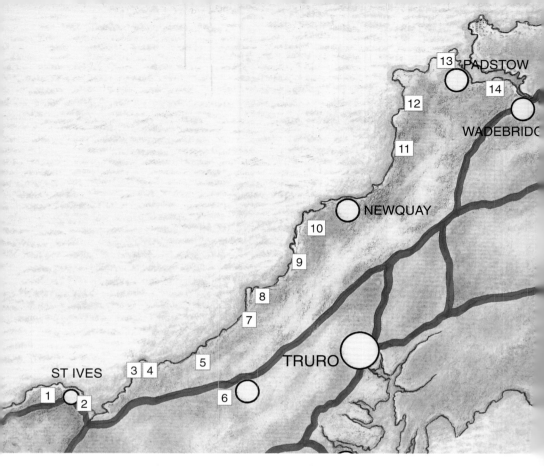

The approximate locations of the walks in this book

This second edition 2012
First published 2006 by
Bossiney Books Ltd, Queens Drive, Ilkley LS29 9QW
www.bossineybooks.com
© 2006 David Wright All rights reserved
ISBN 978-1-906474-38-6

Acknowledgements
The maps are by Graham Hallowell.
Cover based on a design by Heards Design Partnership.
The photographs on pages 1, 9 (lower), 17, 21, 25 and 27 are by the author.
Other photographs are from the publishers' own collection.
The boots on the front cover were kindly supplied by The Brasher Boot Company.

Printed in Great Britain by R Booth Ltd, Penryn, Cornwall

Introduction

A 'shortish' walk is typically 6-8km (4-5 miles) in length, and likely to take 2-3 hours. How long you actually take will depend on your fitness, the weather conditions, and how much you find to interest you along the way. All except one of the walks are circular, mostly involving a stretch of coast path and an inland return.

The area covered includes some of Cornwall's finest beaches and the resort of Newquay, as well as popular coastal towns and villages, but even at peak holiday times the general impression is one of tranquillity and of magnificent coastal scenery, backed by farmland.

The walks may be shortish, but some of them are quite tough going in places, especially on the cliff path. On a few walks you will find a strenuous ascent or two, and uneven walking, but this stretch of the north coast is less demanding than either the Land's End area or North Cornwall and some of the walks are (relatively!) flat and easy.

Proper walking boots are vital for grip and ankle support and a walking pole or stick is useful for balance in the descents. On the inland sections even in dry weather you will find muddy patches, not to mention briars, thistles, gorse and nettles, so bare legs are a liability.

Safety – a real issue for walkers in this area

Cliff walking can be very exposed: the wind-chill factor is like being out in the Atlantic, and Cornish weather can change very rapidly. You need extra layers of clothing, as well as waterproofs, for what is often an abrupt change of temperature between inland and cliff walking.

The most obvious hazard is the cliff path. It is not fenced off from the drop so caution is needed in places. Cliff falls are not uncommon. Walk no nearer the edge than you have to, follow any diversions, and keep a close eye on children and dogs. Don't walk cliff paths in a gale, and don't venture out on the rocks if the sea is rough.

The former mining industry provides much interest and character to some of the walks, but also unique dangers. Stick closely to the paths in these areas and keep dogs on leads.

The maps provided in this book look very attractive but they are only sketch maps, so you may well want to carry the OS 1:25000 map.

The Cornish countryside

Despite many pressures, Cornish farmers are still trying to make a living from the land you are passing through. Please respect crops, leave gates open or shut as you find them, and keep dogs under control when near sheep, especially in the lambing season.

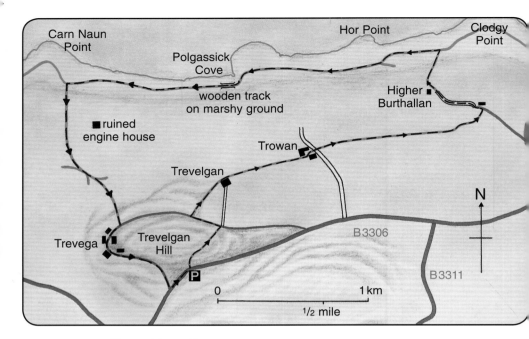

Walk 1 Trevalgan

Distance: 8.3km (5 1/4 miles) Time: 2 1/2 hours
Character: Characteristic West Penwith farmland, then coast path.
The going is tough in places on the coast path and there are several
steep climbs, but it is a lovely and rewarding walk.

Start from a small car park on the B3306 at SW 487396. Coming
from St Ives, this is 2km (1.2 miles) west of the junction with the
B3311, at the top of an incline and just before a bend sign.

Cross the road and climb up and over Trevalgan Hill. The path
terminates at a metal gate. Turn sharp left onto the lane. Opposite
the fourth telegraph pole, turn sharp right on a footpath which has
a wooden waymark post. Go through a gate, then after 10m turn
left over a stile and through fields to Trevalgan Farm. Once there,
use the stile next to the gate and, keeping the farm buildings on
your right, cross a field to another stile.

Follow the path over several stiles and fields, some marked with
the remnants of old black and white posts, to a track of mud and
stone. Here a wooden waymark offers three choices: go straight
ahead over a granite stile into a narrow lane through bushes.

4

It emerges into a field. After 10m cross a stile on the left. Descend to the bottom left-hand corner of the field. Another stile leads to a third field. Head for the gate straight ahead and turn left just before reaching it. Follow the narrow path via a small metal gate and a stile into a field. Keep the hedge on your left and cross the broad stile in the first corner of the field.

The path leads to a lane. Turn left. The lane soon loses its tarmac, becoming a meandering track through fields. Just beyond the entrance to Higher Burthallan, waymarks lead to the coast path.

On reaching it, turn left and enjoy 2.5km of fantastic coastal scenery. Near Polgassick Cove a wooden track leads over marshy ground. Somebody has placed notices on poles topped by tiny spheres. Don't veer from the coast path as suggested.

The path rises towards Carn Naun Point. As the ascent nears its peak, with a ruined engine house to the left, leave the coast path by turning left over a wooden stile.

Follow the path through thorn bushes, fields and a track to a grassy crossroads. Keep left at this point, keeping to the PUBLIC BRIDLEWAY and ignoring footpaths until you reach a quiet country lane. Turn right, following the lane through Trevega and back to the busy B3306. Turn left and walk 100 metres up to the car park.

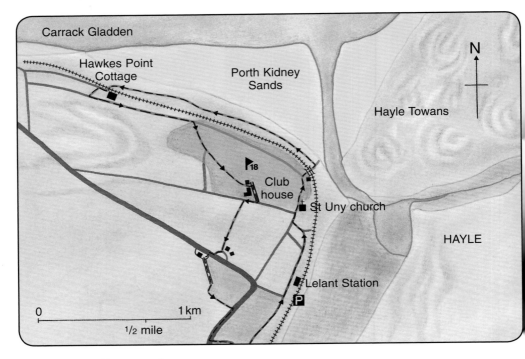

Walk 2   Lelant

Distance: 6.2km (3³/₄ miles)   Time: 1¹/₂ hours
Character: A short and fairly easy walk with lovely views over the
Hayle estuary and Porth Kidney Sands. The inland leg includes a
golf course and agricultural land.

Park at Lelant Station (as distinct from Lelant Saltings Station)
where there is a café which serves cream teas. Even better, make
this a day out by train and give the car a holiday. From the station
car park (SW 548372) turn right on the tarmac lane and follow it,
keeping right at a junction, then curving left to a triangular junction. Turn right, and head towards the church of St Uny.

Take the PUBLIC FOOTPATH CARBIS BAY past the church, crossing a
track at the end of the churchyard. The path leads through the West
Cornwall Golf Course, to a wartime pillbox with a waymark next to
it. Bear right, under the railway, and immediately turn left (COAST
PATH). Stay on this for a kilometre or so, till it leaves the marram
grass dunes, begins to narrow and meanders up through a line of
beech trees, their growth impeded by salt winds from the Atlantic.

6

After a steady climb on a tarmac footpath, gates to the left allow you to cross the railway. Turn right at the entrance to Hawkes Point Cottage. About 20m up the hill, turn left up steps. When you reach the top, turn left again (PUBLIC FOOTPATH). Pass through a kissing gate then keep straight on parallel to the coast. After 500m, another kissing gate gives access again to the golf course.

Cross the gravel path and head uphill to the teeing off point of the 17th hole. From here, signs and white stones guide you over the golf course and just to the left of the club house. Turn right along the club's driveway to leave the golf club grounds, and turn right along the road. After 60m, turn left over a stile onto a PUBLIC FOOTPATH. Keep the hedge on your left over four fields, when you will reach a crescent of tarmac alongside the busy A3074.

Turn right along the crescent, then cross the main road to an agricultural yard almost opposite. Keep left within the yard and enter a well defined track bordered with fences. Follow the track, which becomes a footpath, to the main road.

Cross the road and turn right, passing two MOUNT PLEASANT street signs. The road veers downhill and left. Look out for a street sign on the other side saying ABBEY HILL. Opposite this sign, turn left along an alleyway which leads into a residential street. Follow this street round to a T-junction. Turn left and follow the lane back to Lelant Station.

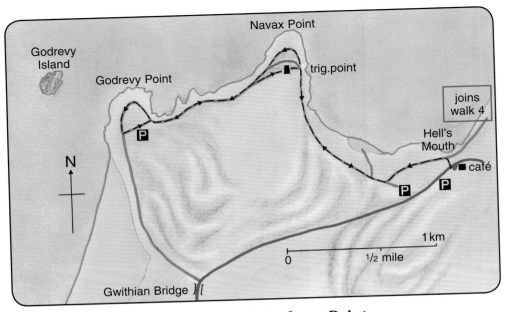

Walk 3 Hell's Mouth and Godrevy Point

Distance: 6.3 km (4 miles) Time: 1 1/2 hours
Character: This is a there-and-back walk, with a loop at the end,
but the scenery is so fine that you will not feel short-changed. The
route passes Mutton Cove, a haven for wild seals, which can often
be seen basking on the shingle beach at low tide. (This section of
the path goes rather near the cliff edge.) The spectacular Godrevy
lighthouse was made famous by Virginia Woolf in her novel 'To the
Lighthouse'. This walk could be combined with Walk 4 as an all-
day outing, using the (seasonal) Hell's Mouth café for a light lunch.

Park at the lay-by (SW 603428) on the Hayle side of the Hell's
Mouth Café, which is on the Hayle-Portreath road. Cross the road
and turn left onto the coast path. Follow the path (ignoring a side
turning on the right, which leads precipitously down to a beach)
to the first headland which is called The Knavocks. You might see
Shetland ponies here, earning their keep by grazing the land.

On the summit of the Knavocks, to your left, you will pass a
stone-built 'trig. point'. Godrevy lighthouse now comes into view.
A lesser path to the right leads around the outside of Navax Point
and then rejoins the main path.

8

Godrevy Island from the Knavocks

Seals on the beach at Mutton Cove

Leave the Knavocks via a kissing gate: the sandy expanses of St Ives Bay soon come into view. This is where St Ia arrived in Cornwall on a cabbage leaf, having sailed from Ireland with God speed. St Ives is named after her. Look out for a grassy path on the left which leads up from a car park. Take a peek over the cliff edge when you reach this path junction: this is Mutton Cove, and if you're lucky you'll see seals lounging on the beach here at low tide.

Continue along the coast path around Godrevy Point, where the view is dominated by Godrevy Island and its lighthouse. Leave the headland across a stile, and immediately turn left. Keep the wall on your left and follow it up to rejoin the coast path above Mutton Cove. Retrace your steps to Hell's Mouth – not forgetting to turn left immediately after passing between stone gateposts.

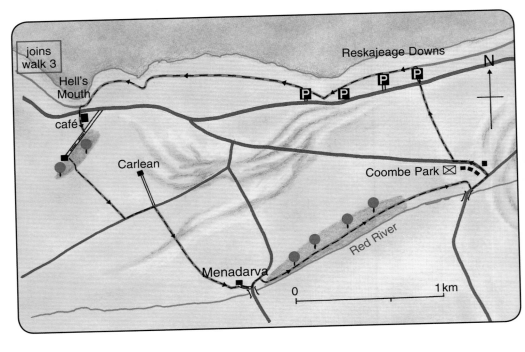

Walk 4 Reskajeage and Hell's Mouth

Distance: 7.5km (4³/₄ miles)   Time: 2¹/₄ hours
*Character: From the dappled light of woodland, broad arable fields
and the soft babbling of the Red River to the dramatic scenery of
Cornwall's north coast – this walk has it all. It is likely to be muddy
in places. Can be combined with Walk 3.*

From Portreath, take the unclassified road towards Hayle and, after
passing Reskajeage Downs, park at any one the cliff-top car parks
before you reach Hell's Mouth Café. Face the Atlantic Ocean and
turn left, following the coast path to Hell's Mouth. This dramatic
65m drop to the ocean and a slate floor lies close to the road.

Cross the road. Walk down the unmarked footpath immediately
beside the right hand wall of the Hell's Mouth Café. A stile leads
down to a track. Turn right along it, with a patch of woodland to
your left, and continue until a house comes into view.

About 15m before you reach the house, take a narrow and sometimes overgrown path on the left. It can be muddy, too, and gets
even muddier as it crosses two little streams. Go through a gate.

10

Keep the hedge on your left as you climb gently through two fields. Arriving at a tarmac lane, turn left and after 200m (opposite the entrance to Carlean) turn right (PUBLIC FOOTPATH) and cross two fields.

At the end of the second field, turn left through a gate, then head diagonally across the third field, heading for the farmyard in the valley beyond the trees. Go through a gate into the farmyard, and veer right down a track just before the farmhouse.

Keep left along the tarmac lane, then after 80m turn right over a stream (PUBLIC BRIDLEWAY). A waymark confirms this is Menadarva. The bridleway turns left along a broad path, flanked by the Red River on the right and a stunted wood on the left.

The catchment area for the Red River includes the old mine areas of Camborne, so it is discoloured by passing through tin and copper ore – though it must have been even redder in the past when the mines were active and its water was used to separate the ore from the waste rock. Now the valley is a nature reserve.

Continue along the main path for 1.5km, when you will reach a tarmac lane. Turn left along it and after 100m left again (HAYLE) The road swings left and begins to rise. Pass several bungalows.

Opposite Coombe Park caravan site, take the PUBLIC FOOTPATH to the right. It rises between trees before farmland vistas open up.

At the top of the hill is a stile. Cross the Portreath-Hayle road into North Cliffs car park, and out to the coast path. Turn left and follow the path back to your car.

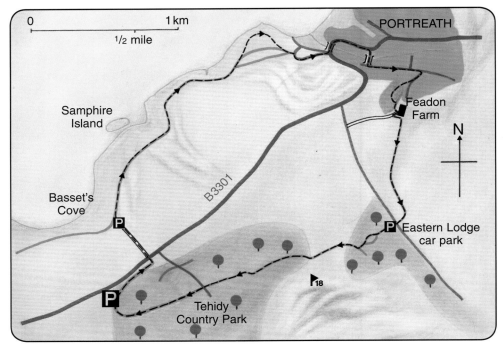

Walk 5 Tehidy

Distance: 7.3 km (4¹/₂ miles)   Time: 2¹/₄ hours
Character: A varied and beautiful walk, with woodland and coast
as well as former industrial port of Portreath. There are several
steep climbs.

Park at East Lodge car park (SW 658440) off Cot Road, in Tehidy
Country Park. Take the middle path from the car park into a long
band of sycamores. The path forks quite a lot and there are many
possible routes through the trees: I went right at the first fork, left
at the second and left again at the third.

Turn right at a T-junction and walk alongside the golf course,
passing the teeing off point for the thirteenth hole. Go straight
ahead (NORTH CLIFFS PLANTATION) at the junction a few metres
beyond tee 13 and follow the pink arrows to North Cliffs car park.
Enjoy the varied woodland of this lovely park. After a delightful
stroll through a forest of silver birch trees turn right into North
Cliffs car park. Walk out of the car park and turn right onto a grass
roadside verge.

12

After about 50 m, the verge peters out. Cross the road and follow the PUBLIC BYWAY towards the sea.

At a roughly circular parking place (Basset's Cove) turn right onto the coast path and follow it to Portreath. There are two consecutive steep valleys on the way, one down to Samphire Island, the other to Porth Cadjack Cove.

If you reach Portreath at low tide you can walk along the sand. Otherwise, turn right up a lane (COAST PATH) which runs above the beach. From the public car park, follow the main road inland, passing the public conveniences, until the road sweeps away to the left. Turn right here across a stream, then left under a low bridge into Glenfeadon Terrace which leads eventually to Primrose Terrace.

Take a sharp right (MINING TRAIL ILLOGAN) at 'Glenfeadon Cottage' to pass castellated 'Glenfeadon Castle', then immediately veer right onto a gently rising PUBLIC FOOTPATH. Follow this path through Feadon Farm and its various wildlife and agricultural attractions. Turn left (PUBLIC FOOTPATH) at the T-junction. After 50 m, turn right onto a tarmac track and follow the signs to Tehidy.

The path leads back to Cot Road, where the car park is almost immediately opposite.

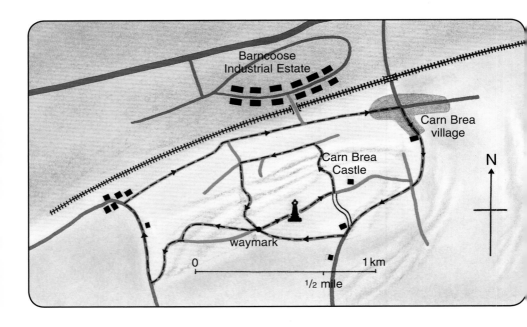

Walk 6   Carn Brea

Distance: 7km (4¹/₄ miles)   Time: 2 hours
Character: Carn Brea is set in the midst of what was once a major
mining area, now replaced in part by light industry. It is a granite
outcrop, with dramatic tors and extensive views, not least of dozens
of old engine houses. The walk has an inner loop which could be
omitted, saving perhaps 600m and a very stiff ascent.

Kerbside parking is available in Carn Brea village – signposted from
the A3047 Redruth-Camborne road. Once through the village,
turn right (dead end) at the crossroads and find somewhere to
park considerately. Head back on foot to the crossroads and turn
right (another dead end). This leads to a PUBLIC FOOTPATH, going
through a kissing gate and past 'Cheri Amor'.

On reaching a 5-way junction, take the second path from the
left. It winds uphill to a junction which is just below a bungalow.
Turn left and follow the boundary fence of the property. Just past
gateposts crowned with horses' heads, turn right along a path. Stay
on this path until you reach a timber waymark. Note this point as
you will return to it later.

Turn right (blue arrow) towards the monumental cross, erected in 1836. The view from here is a remarkable mix of old and new, of toil and leisure. Continue east towards Carn Brea Castle to a granite edged layby.

You can now choose whether to retrace your steps to the wooden waymark, or to undertake the inner circuit of the walk.

For the inner circuit, take the mud path to the left a few metres beyond the layby, which descends steeply. Keep to the narrow but obvious main path through a gulley. At the bottom of the hill turn left at the T-junction to walk westward alongside Carn Brea. Keep right at a junction, then turn left at a crossing of paths, to head uphill – the path becomes steep and rocky – to the wooden way-mark. Turn right towards the tors on the western end of Carn Brea.

The main path can be picked up just to the south of the most westerly outcrop. Follow it downhill to a T-junction. Turn right onto the tarmac track. Descend, keeping to the track and ignoring footpath signs, to a waymark signed GREAT FLAT LODE TRAIL. Turn right here past 'Sans Souci'.

The path soon becomes tarmac, and leads back to the starting point of the walk.

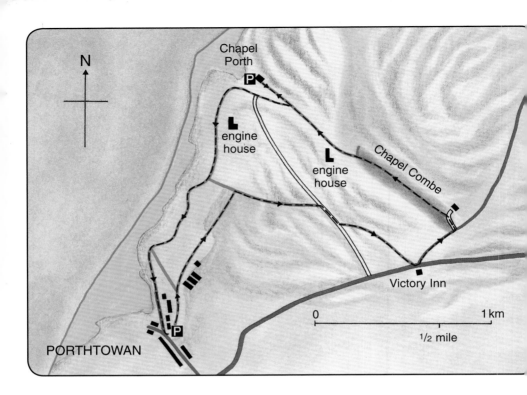

Walk 7   Porthtowan, Chapel Combe & Chapel Porth

Distance: 5.5 km (3 1/2 miles)   Time: 1 1/2 hours
Character: A varied and beautiful walk, and with no stiles and relatively easy gradients given the hilly country covered. The cliff-top section provides evidence of both farming and historic mining activity, whilst along Chapel Combe there is attractive woodland, and the air is heavy with the scent of seasonal wild flowers. A visit to Chapel Porth adds about 600 m to the walk, and it is an alternative starting place.

Climb the steps at the rear of Porthtowan beach car park (SW693480) and walk up the middle (and steepest) of three paths. Pass – or pause at – the seaward-facing bench and keep left when the path forks just below the second bench. About 50m further on, take the right hand path, which climbs parallel to houses. Ignore the minor paths which cross it. After skirting a field you will reach a rural crossroads. Turn right.

After 400m, an old mine track joins the path from the left. Keep walking inland. Wooden posts warn of the dangers arising from old mine workings. As you draw level with the most inland of these posts, bear left onto a muddier track which branches off, and leads directly to the Victory Inn. Turn left onto the road outside the inn, then left again down a lane towards Trenerry Farm and Mingoose.

Before reaching the valley floor, take the PUBLIC BRIDLEWAY to the left. When the path veers right towards dwellings and becomes tarmac, carry straight on along the footpath. Relax into the magic of Chapel Combe, where birdsong mingles with the music of an unseen brook. Just before you reach a ruined engine house, keep left at a junction. A stone bridge carries you across a smudge of marsh and a mining scar and the well defined path meanders down to a waymark post at a junction.

For Chapel Porth – a delightful cove and beach where you'll find toilets and a seasonal café – carry straight on for a further 300m. Then return to this point.

Alternatively, turn left and climb steadily up the incline of Mulgram Hill. This is part of the coast path, marked by acorn waymarks,. Follow it back to Porthtowan. Descending to the cove at Porthtowan, continue inland past cafés and beach shops until you reach the car park.

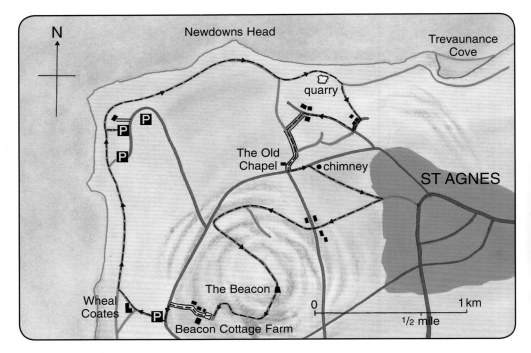

Walk 8 St Agnes Beacon

Distance: 8.3km (5 1/4 miles)   Time: 2 1/4 hours
Character: This lovely and varied walk in what was once a major
tin mining area features panoramic views from the Beacon,
pleasant farmland, the ruins of Wheal Coates tin mine, and some
attractive cliff scenery.

Park at St Agnes Head in the car park near the lookout station
(SW700513). Head towards the sea and turn right when you reach
the coastal path. Go past Newdowns Head and a fork in the track.
Continue along the coast path to a small disused quarry. Beyond
the quarry, leave the coast path by turning right at a fork. Turn
right again at a junction, and head up towards a white bungalow.

Turn right along the road, pass 'Little Polberrow' and head for
the footpath signs. The direct route straight ahead through the old
mine workings is not a right of way, so turn right along the lane,
then after passing 'Atlantic Beacon' turn left along a broad track.
This bears left. At the next junction keep left and follow the track
to 'The Old Chapel'. Turn left onto the road.

18

Turn right just before reaching the chimney. The track takes you past the chimney to a stile into a field. A diagonal path leads over the field to a track at its bottom left corner. This track, then path, then track again, leads to a T-junction.

Turn right (THE BEACON) and follow the path over more fields to a lane. Cross the lane and take the footpath opposite (TO THE BEACON). This guides you around the Beacon, rising at first, then descending to a lane. Turn sharp left here up the track and keep climbing until you reach the top of the Beacon, 189 m above sea level.

Take the path heading in the direction of Redruth and Camborne. Keep to the main path as you descend. At a junction of five paths, bear right which after 50 m brings you to a gate, to the right of which is a stile. Cross the stile and keep the hedge on your right to walk round the perimeter of the field to a gate near a standing stone. Go through the gate and through a concrete yard towards buildings, then follow the gated drive of Beacon Cottage Farm (a rather attractive and discreet caravan site) out to a road.

Turn left and after 100 m turn right at Wheal Coates car park. Follow the main path from the far end of the car park into the preserved remains of Wheal Coates, where an information board gives a fascinating insight into the area's industrial history.

From Wheal Coates, turn right onto the coast path and follow it back past Tubby's Head to your car.

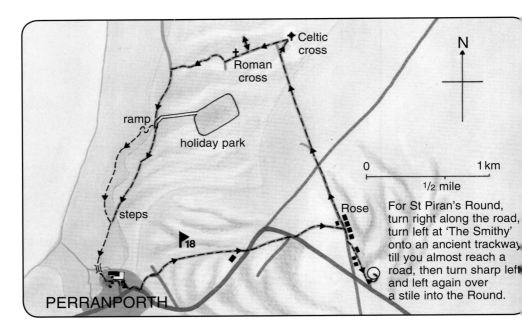

For St Piran's Round, turn right along the road, turn left at 'The Smithy' onto an ancient trackway till you almost reach a road, then turn sharp left and left again over a stile into the Round.

Walk 9   Perranporth

Distance: 7.3km (4 1/2 miles) Time: 2 1/4 hours
Character: St Piran, patron saint of Cornwall and of tinners, lived in the dunes which feature in this walk and which overwhelmed two successive churches. You can extend the walk to include St Piran's Round, a medieval amphitheatre, adding 1km.

To reach the start of the walk, take the B3285 from Goonhavern towards Perranporth. After 1.4 miles, when the main road bends left, turn right on an unclassified road (MOUNT/TREBELLAN) and park in the layby opposite the first right turn (SW775554).

Head onto the dunes by way of a kissing gate and take the right fork. The path is way-marked by a combination of white stones and wooden posts marked with a black acorn. At length a holed (Celtic) cross comes in view, ahead and to the right. Keep going until you come to a fork. Bear right, towards the cross, which marks the site of an eleventh century church.

From this cross, head towards the Roman cross crowning a sand dune to the south-west. This commemorates the site of the buried St Piran's Oratory – the original sixth century church. Continue in the same direction for a few metres, then turn right on a well-defined path that crosses a footbridge before rising gently through more dunes. Keep to the main path which gradually makes its way towards the sea until the coast path crosses it.

Turn left onto the coast path which eventually descends to Perranporth beach. Along the way there are various points of access to the beach which can be used, tide permitting, as alternative routes.

Head towards Perranporth. Cross a bridge over a little stream, then take a few stone steps up onto a miniature promenade.

Turn left across a grassy area: between the second bungalow and a house there is an alleyway which takes you up a few steps, past 'Tremeer' and to the car park of Ponsmere Hotel. Turn immediately right down a lane. Just beyond the museum turn left into a lane called Eureka Vale, and then left again along the main road.

Just before the pavement runs out, turn left (PUBLIC FOOTPATH) up steps. Turn right at the top and then cross a track onto a footpath which leads into Perranporth Golf Club. The route is marked by white stones. Cross a tarmac track in front of the clubhouse and continue up to the main road. Great care is needed here as it's a blind bend. Cross the road to a stile, then cross the field diagonally, heading to a stile to the left of some floodlit pitches. Walk on behind the pitch to another stile.

Cross the road and take PUBLIC FOOTPATH ROSE, through gorse and blackthorn bushes. Enter a field by a kissing gate and keep the hedge close on your right to a gate, which brings you to the village of Rose. You could turn left and follow the road back to the lay-by where you started, or visit St Piran's Round (see map).

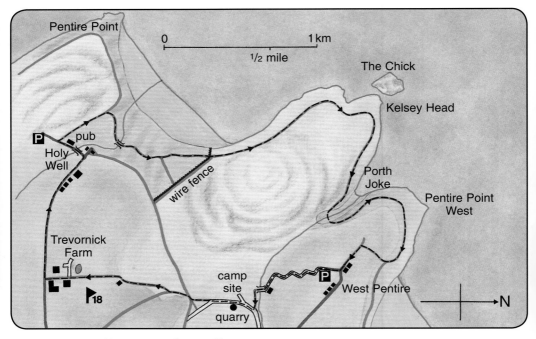

Walk 10   Holy Well to West Pentire

Distance: 8.2km (5 miles)   Time: 2 hours
Character: A short stretch of dunes, then cliffs with stunning beach and sea views, then a short inland return. The walk can be started either from Holy Well or from the car park at West Pentire: our directions assume the former. There are two pubs, shops and public toilets at Holy Well, which may affect your decision.

Starting from the National Trust car park at Holy Well (SW 767587), turn right along the footpath towards the beach, which passes St Piran's Inn. After 200m take a right fork to cross a wooden bridge. Carry straight on (acorn waymark) over a series of dunes. The coast path runs roughly parallel to the sea, but sand moves about and the path is not always clear. It leaves the dunes at a kissing gate quite near the cliff edge. If you reach a wire fence higher up, turn left down it and you'll come to the kissing gate.

From the kissing gate go straight ahead following a well defined cliff path round to the finger-like cove of Porth Joke. The stream over the beach can be crossed by a bridge. Once through another kissing gate, turn left and walk above the eastern side of Porth Joke

to Pentire Point West. As you turn inland, Crantock Beach comes into view, with the valley of the River Gannell funnelling inland. At the next kissing gate take the right fork. Turn left at a T-junction. Another kissing gate leads to the village of West Pentire.

After 100m turn right (PUBLIC FOOTPATH) up a lane which leads to a car park – the alternative starting point. From here it becomes a track, meandering downhill through farmland before reaching the valley floor.

The footpath is clearly marked over a stream and alongside a camping field, before reaching yet another kissing gate. Turn right onto the track and fork left to rise gently past a small disused quarry. When the path forks, bear right on a grassy path towards a five-barred gate at the low point of a fenced enclosure.

Several paths meet at the gate. Go straight ahead, keeping the fence on your left for 50m before bearing away to the right, cutting the corner to a Cornish hedge. Pass to the right of a house at the end of this path, to a gate then a second gate, entering a golf course.

Follow the path through the golf course, and keep left at the pond, going straight ahead through Trevornick Farm with its holiday facilities to emerge onto a road. Turn right, and follow the footway back down to Holy Well, passing the Treguth Inn and then St Piran's Inn.

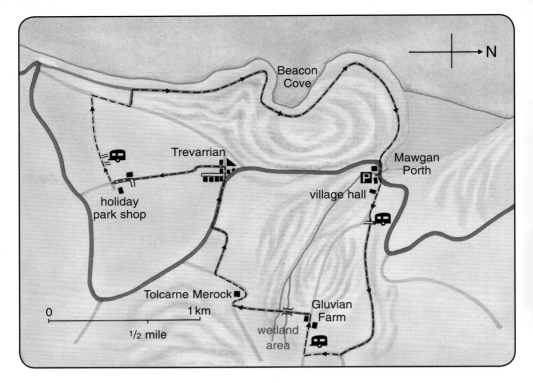

Walk 11 Mawgan Porth

Distance: 8.2km (5 miles)   Time: 2¹/₄ hours
Character: The coastal path between Watergate Bay and Mawgan
Porth is both charming and dramatic, but we start with an inland
section of rolling green fields, and an area of wetland to add interest
for naturalists.

Start at Mawgan Porth from the car park next to Betty's shop. Turn
right on leaving the car park, then right again (MAWGAN) to pass
the village hall. After about 250m bear left on PUBLIC BRIDLEWAY.

The path soon crosses the entrance to a holiday park. Keep right
for MAWGAN at a junction.

The path joins a lane beyond a caravan park. Carry on up the hill
and turn right at the T-junction, past Gluvian Farm. Just beyond
Gluvian farmyard on the left, take a track on the left: a triangular
FORD sign can be seen poking out of the vegetation. There is a footbridge next to the ford. This is a wetland area, and there is a further
stream to be crossed before the path rises into the trees.

Join a quiet tarmac lane which circles round an impressive granite farmhouse. Near the top of the hill, turn right (PUBLIC FOOTPATH) over a stile. Keep the hedge on your right to another stile at the end of the field. A delightful grassy footpath leads out to a road. Turn right, and follow the road for 250 m to Trevarrian.

Bear left at a 'no entry' sign and follow the street ahead for 60 m, then turn left, PUBLIC FOOTPATH. Keep left, apparently up a bungalow drive, but the path keeps to the left through a narrow gate. A stile leads into a field. Keep the hedge on your left: it turns left, then you turn immediately right across a gap, again with the hedge on your left.

Follow it for one and a half sides of this field, then cross a stile. Now keep the hedge on your right (including a right then left turn) till you reach a stile on your right. Cross, turn left towards the farmyard and exit via the stile to the left of the gate.

Go forward up the farm track to a road junction. Turn right here, opposite the Watergate Bay Holiday Park's shop, and continue along this road to a T-junction. Turn right here – but be careful: this road is fairly busy in season.

At the top of the rise a kissing gate on the left leads to the coast path. Turn right and follow the coast path back to Mawgan Porth.

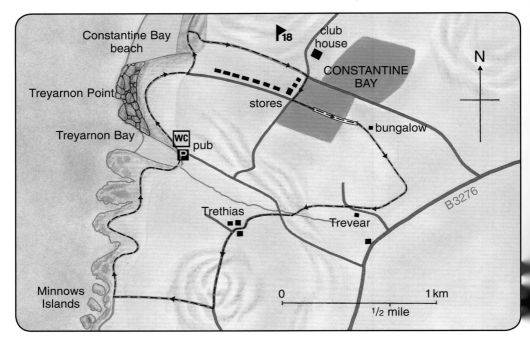

Walk 12 Treyarnon

Distance: 8km (5 miles) Time: 2 hours
Character: Starting from the popular cove at Treyarnon, this walk
takes in a view of Constantine Bay and its dunes before heading
inland through farmland, then returning to the coast for some of
Cornwall's most extraordinary cliff scenery. It's an easy walk, with
stiles but no serious ascents or descents.

Treyarnon lies west of St Merryn and is signed off the B3276.
From the car park alongside Treyarnon Bay (SW 859740), head
past the public toilets towards the coast path and turn right along
it. Rounding Treyarnon Point, the path heads briefly inland (acorn
waymark). Walk past the metal gate at the entrance to the broad
beach of Constantine Bay, and 10m further on turn left on a narrow path into the dunes. About halfway along the bay, turn right
and up steps on a path which then skirts a golf course.

On reaching a road, with the clubhouse to your left, turn right
onto a grass-verged road. Constantine Bay Stores lies 150m ahead.
Turn left opposite the Stores along a private residential road signed
as a PUBLIC FOOTPATH.

The road – intermittently metalled – leads to Pops Close and beyond it to an isolated white bungalow. Pass to the right of the bungalow, to a stile, and into a field beyond. Keep the hedge on your left across this and three further fields.

The fourth field has an open gateway at the end of its first side. Go through the gap and turn right, keeping the hedge on your right and following it round to a gateway. The exit point from the next field may sometimes be overgrown. It is in the far left corner, and a stile delivers you onto a lane. Turn right along the lane, past Trevear Cottage.

After 100 m, when the road veers right, bear left onto PUBLIC FOOTPATH. Cross two fields. In the third field the path forks. Bear left to cross a stream, then turn right along the hedge, to a stile 10 m up from the corner. Turn right into a lane, and immediately left at a junction. Keeping to the lane, pass through Trethias Farm and ignore a side turning. After 500 m, at the top of a rise, turn right on a permissive footpath out to the coast path.

You could now turn right to return directly, but if you turn left and walk another 500 m along the coast path (as far as a waymark which, rather unnecessarily, suggests you change course) you will be rewarded with some spectacular erosion scenery.

Now retrace your steps and the coast path will lead you back to Treyarnon Bay.

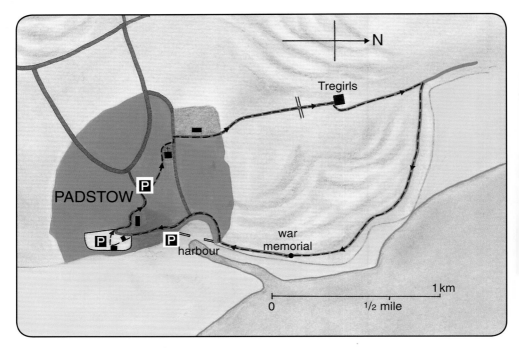

Walk 13   Padstow

Distance: 5.5km (3 1/2 miles)   Time: 1 1/2 hours
Character: A short and fairly easy walk, with no really steep ascents
and just three stiles. It tracks through the one-time fishing port of
Padstow, now famed as the home of celebrity chef Rick Stein, and
includes a sweep of the coastal path offering splendid views of the
Camel estuary.

Entering Padstow by the A39, turn off the main road for TOWN
CENTRE/DOCKS and turn left into the Lawn car park, clearly signed
(SW918753). Follow the TOURIST INFORMATION sign near a children's play area, which leads you down steps to a path. Turn left.
The wooded path leads to a lych gate at the entrance to the churchyard of St Petroc's. Follow the path to the left of the church and
leave the churchyard by turning left up Church Street.

Take the first on the right which is Tregirls Lane. Walk past
Prideaux Place. Pass under an arch on which a sign warns TREGIRLS
FARM VEHICLES ACCESS ONLY. This metalled road, flanked by hedges
which in Spring are alive with campion, primroses and bluebells,

28

leads to Tregirls Farm. On the boundary of the farmyard, just beside a barn, there's a stile on the right. Cross, and enjoy the wonderful view of the Camel estuary. Turn left down the track to the coast path, marked by a wooden post with an acorn logo on its far side.

Turn right along the coast path, which will take you back towards Padstow. At length you will reach Padstow's war memorial. Take the left fork beyond it, and follow the path into the town. Keep close to the quayside, following it round to The Old Customs House pub where the road veers right, passing Rick Stein's Seafood Restaurant.

Padstow's station car park, further up the road, must be amongst the most interesting car parks in the country! Turn left into it. The long two-storey building to your right houses Rick Stein's delicatessen, his fish and chip shop and his school of cookery.

A similar looking building to the left is the National Lobster Hatchery, where seeded female lobsters find nurturing respite from the harsh vagaries of the wild in order to give their unborn young a better chance of survival.

Turn right as you draw alongside the hatchery entrance and leave the car park past the old station and up Station Road. Walk past the Metropole Hotel and, at the road junction, follow the main road (WADEBRIDGE) and then after 50m turn right into the car park.

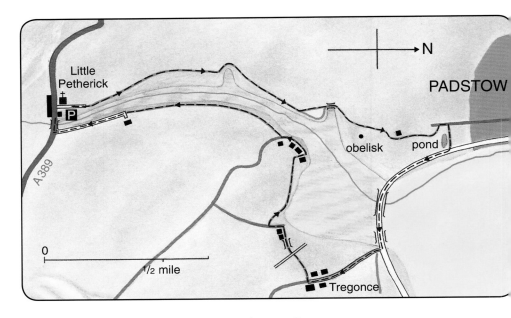

Walk 14   Little Petherick Creek

Distance: 7.5km (4³/₄ miles)   Time: 2¹/₄ hours
Character: A beautiful and varied walk, with creek scenery quite
unlike any other walk in this book. Because part of the circuit,
about three-quarters way round, includes a path within reach
of the tide, you need to check before you go that you will not be
walking there near the time of high water. Parts of the walk can
be quite muddy.

Little Petherick lies between Wadebridge and Padstow on the
A389. There's a car park behind the village hall, between the bridge
and the church (SW918722).

Turn right out of the car park along the lane and past a row of
modern cottages. Follow the Saints' Way waymarks, identified by a
stylised cross. We shall follow this well-signed long-distance path
out to the Camel Trail. It twists and turns as it rises first through
woodland, then fields, before crossing two small creeks.

After a bridge over the second creek, climb steeply to a ridge,
aiming about 200m to the left of the obelisk. Turn right over a
stile and immediately left down the side of a field to a metal gate.
Continue down the track past Dennis Farm to a T-junction. Turn

30

right onto Dennis Cove Lake Area and skirt a large pond. Just before you reach the far end of the pond, steps ahead of you lead up to the Camel Trail – a busy cyclepath.

Turn right and cross the mouth of Little Petherick Creek by a box girder bridge, then a second more modest bridge. Some 50 m further on, turn right, PERMISSIVE FOOTPATH ONLY. Follow the track up to Tregonce. Opposite Tregonce farmhouse, turn right onto PUBLIC FOOTPATH. Cross two fields. Leave the second field by a wooden kissing gate, cross the track and go through another metal gate almost opposite. Descend the field to a bridge, near houses.

Pass the first house then turn left (signed F/P) and walk uphill to a sign PUBLIC FOOTPATH SEA MILLS. Turn sharp right through the gate of 'Benuick', then turn left up clearly marked steps to a stile. Cross the stile and turn right. Keep the hedge on your right across two and a half fields, then take a stile on the right which leads into a narrow footpath alongside a house, and out to the quayside.

Turn left along the quayside, passing several houses, then take the PUBLIC FOOTPATH LITTLE PETHERICK which bears off to the right along the shore of the creek. This is where the path is liable to flooding at high tide. Follow the path until it peters out, at a point where an incline to the left, with a sign at the top PUBLIC FOOTPATH SEA MILLS, leads up to a grassy river-bank walk.

Turn right here, and follow the path over stiles and footbridges back to Little Petherick. Turn right on to the main road to cross the bridge, then right again into the car park.

Some other Bossiney walks books

Shortish walks – Bodmin Moor (5-9 km walks)
Shortish walks in north Cornwall (5-8 km walks)
Shortish walks near the Land's End (5-8 km walks)
Shortish walks on and around The Lizard (6-8 km walks)
Shortish walks – Lower Tamar Valley (5-8 km walks)
Shortish walks – Truro to Looe (5-9 km walks)
Pub Walks – Padstow to Hartland (9-14 km walks
Really short walks – North Cornwall (3-5 km walks)

Shortish walks on Dartmoor (5-8 km walks)
Shortish walks in north Devon (5-9 km walks)
Shortish walks – The South Devon Coast (6-9 km walks)
Shortish walks – Torbay and Dartmouth (5-9 km walks)

For a full list of our walks books covering Cornwall, Devon
and much of Somerset, please see our website:
www.bossineybooks.com